The Print Handwriting Workbook for Kids

For general information on our other products and services or to obtain technical support, please contact our Customer Care Department within the United States at (866) 744-2665, or outside the United States at (510) 253-0500.

Zephyros Press publishes its books in a variety of electronic and print formats. Some content that appears in print may not be available in electronic books, and vice versa.

Interior and Cover Designer: Kristine Brogno
Editor: Lia Brown
Production Editor: Erum Khan

Author photo: Twenty Toes Photography

ISBN: Print 978-1-64152-418-6

Printed in Canada

The Print Handwriting
WORKBOOK for KIDS

Laugh, Learn, and **Practice** **Print** with **Jokes and Riddles**

Crystal Radke

ZEPHYROS PRESS

Note to Parents

Being able to write letters is very important for young children. It helps them to remember and recall letters in words when learning to read. Handwriting also engages the brain in a different way than when we type them on a keyboard or touch them on a screen.

By working through this book, your child will:

- Grow their visual motor skills such as hand-eye coordination.

- Increase their working memory abilities.

- Strengthen their fine motor skills.

- Have increased reading fluency due to a better visual perception of letters.

To help your child be successful, we have formatted this book in sections. First, they will learn each letter, starting with capital letters and moving on to lowercase letters. Then, they will learn to combine those letters and write words. Lastly, they will write jokes using the skills previously learned.

We hope you find this book helpful in teaching your child to write in print and that your child enjoys working through its pages!

Trace and Write Letters

▲▽▲▽▲▽▲▽▲▽▲▽▲▽▲▽▲▽▲▽▲▽▲▽▲▽▲▽▲▽▲

DIRECTIONS

This section will teach you how to write each letter of the alphabet in print. Each page will teach you a new letter. We will start with capital letters and then learn to write lowercase letters.

For the best results, complete this workbook in order. Take your time and complete every page. Sit in your chair with your feet flat on the ground and under the table. Practice using proper pencil grasp.

Pay attention to the first letter on each page that includes numbers and arrows. This shows you exactly how you should begin to write the letter and the order of your pencil strokes.

First, you will trace the dotted letters. Then, practice writing your letters on your own. You are on your way to writing in print!

Happy writing!

What do alligators drink before a race?
Gator-Ade!

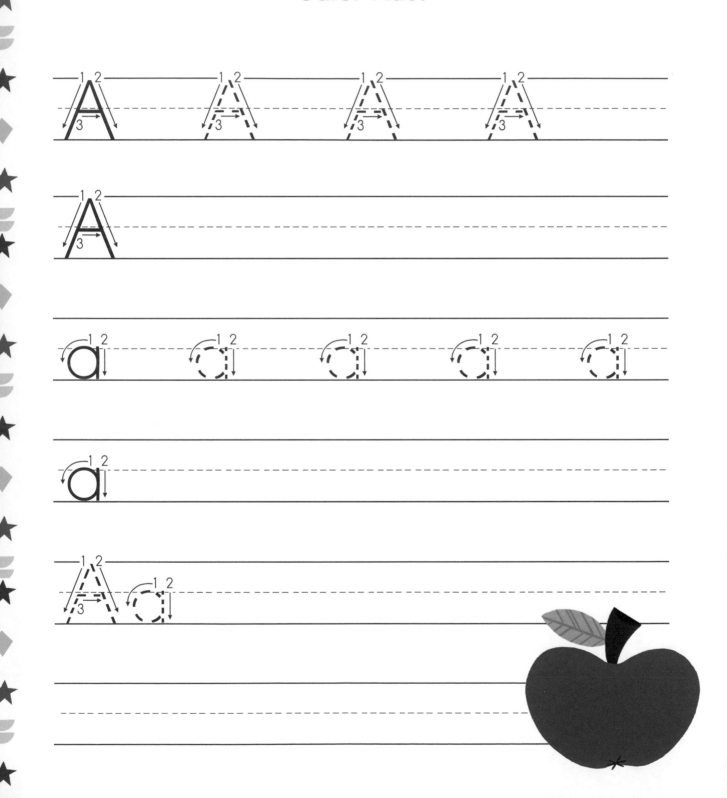

What do planets like to read?
Comet books!

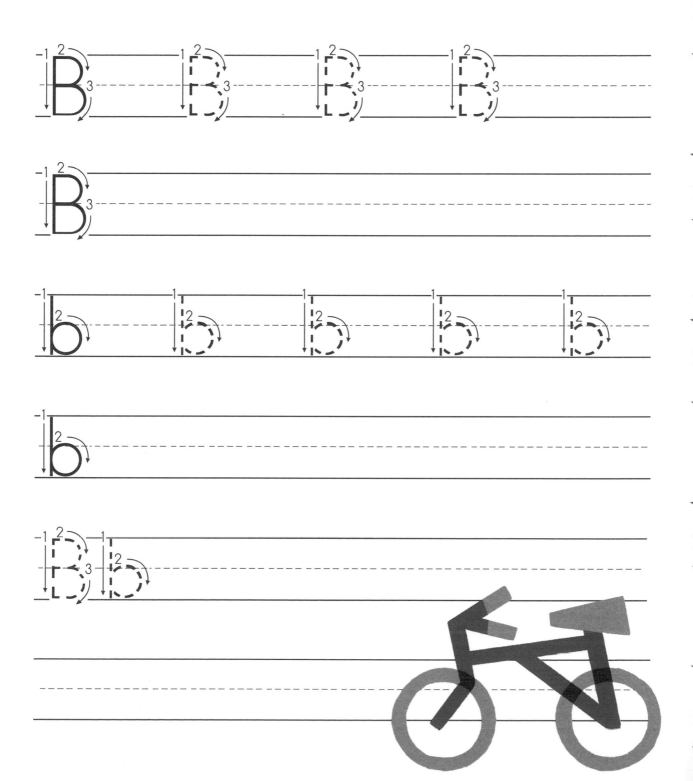

Why was the clown sad?
He broke his funny bone!

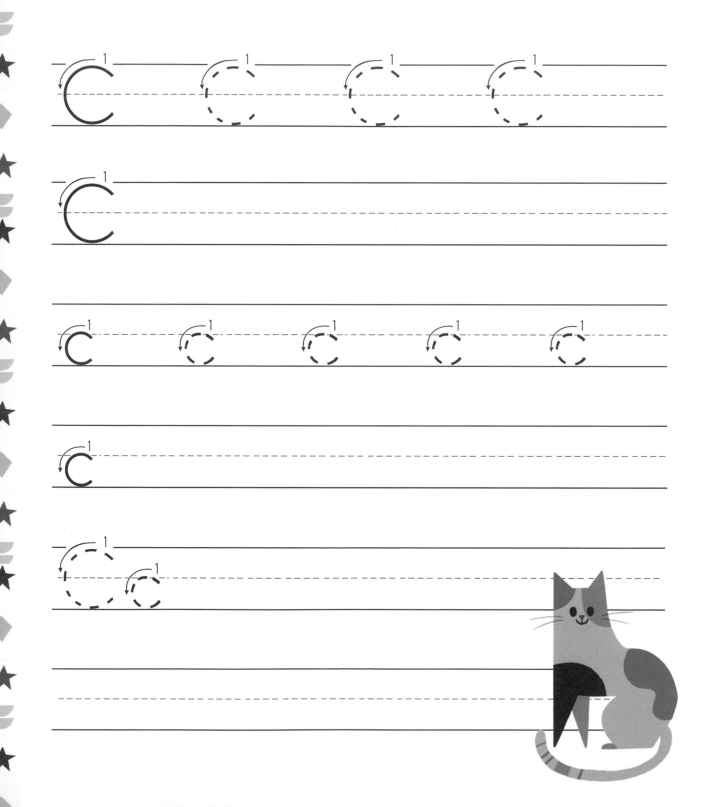

What does a dragon eat for a snack?
Firecrackers!

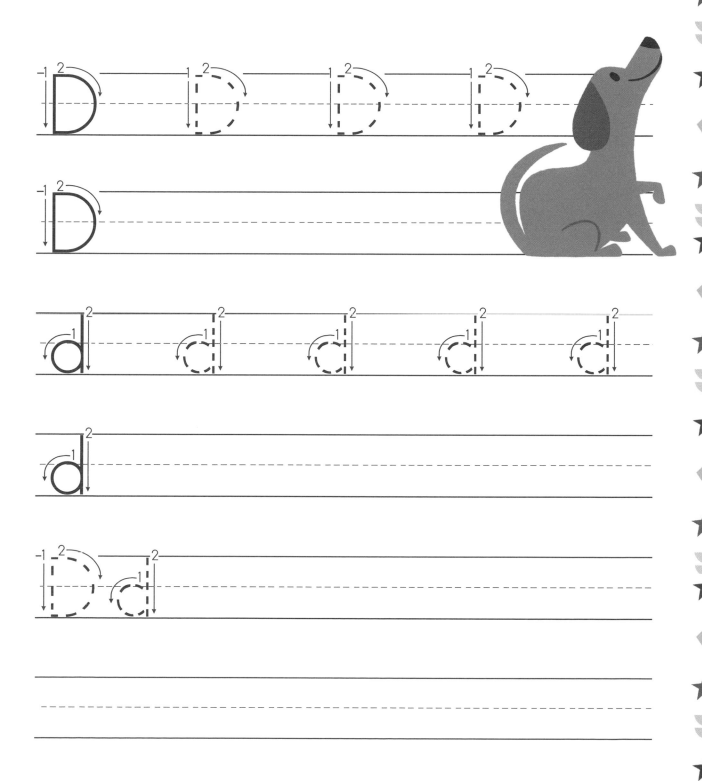

What did the egg say to the clown?
You crack me up!

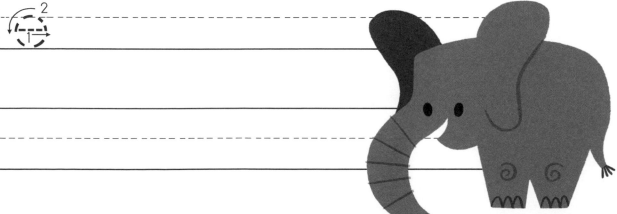

Why didn't the fly land on the computer?
It was afraid of the world wide web!

Why did the grape stop in the middle of the road?
Because he ran out of juice!

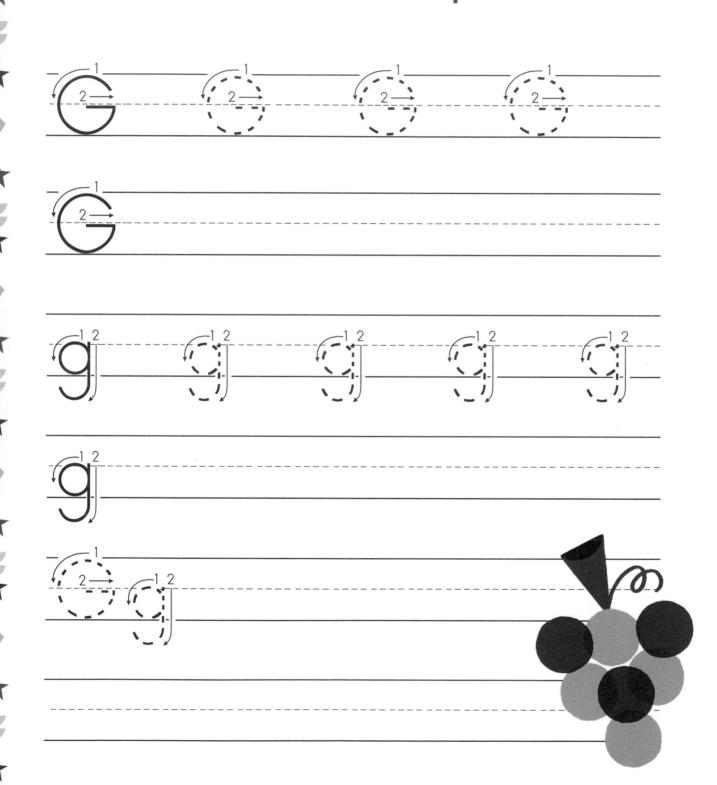

What's a hippo's favorite type of music?
Hip-hop!

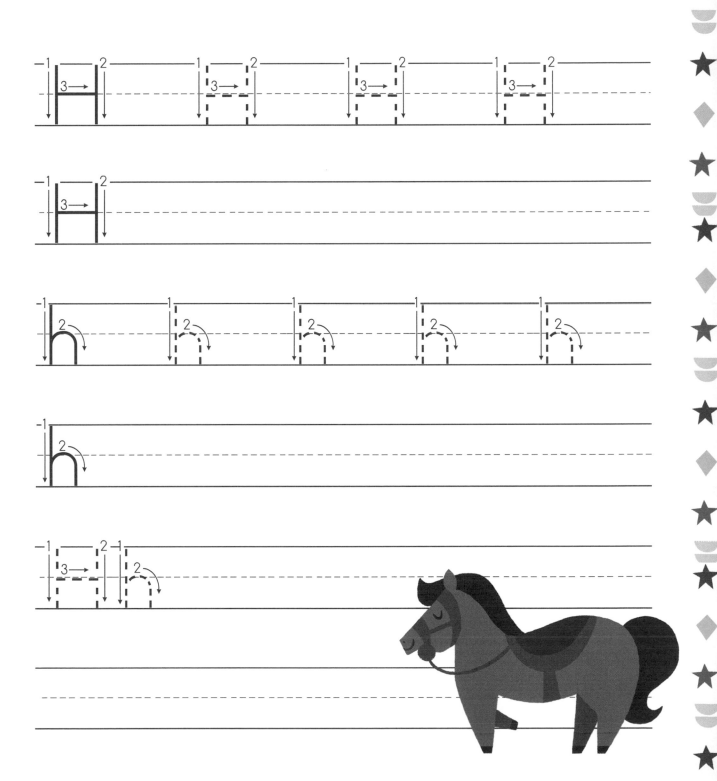

What did the newspaper say to the ice cream?
What's the scoop?

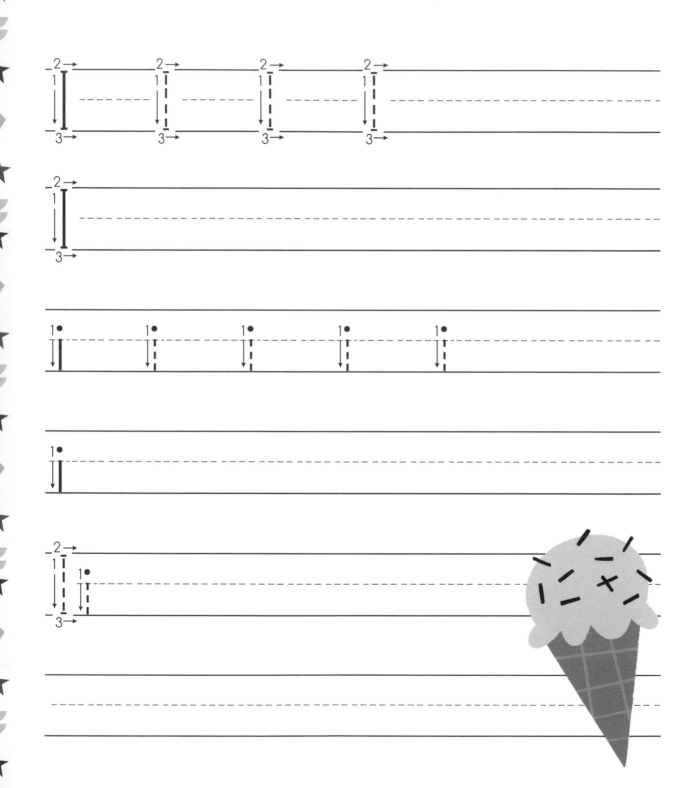

What kind of fish goes well with peanut butter?
Jelly fish!

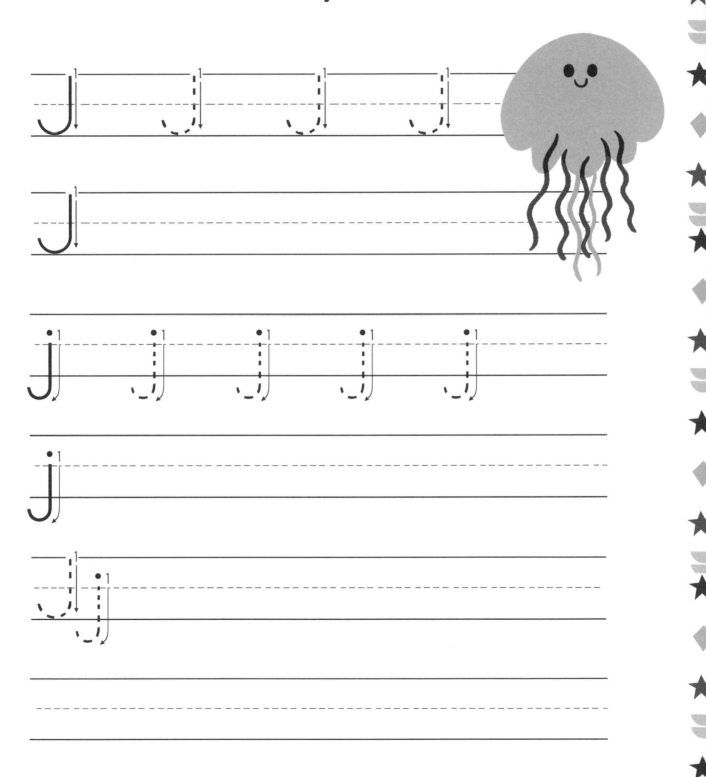

What did the king say to the dentist?
I came to get my crown!

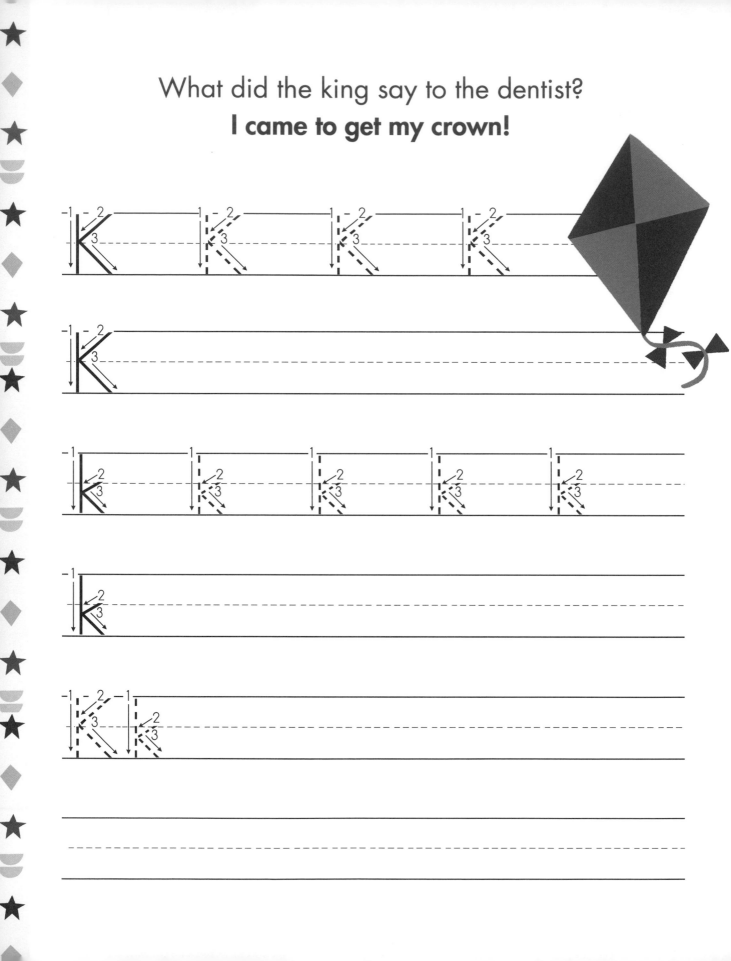

What do you call a lion's reflection?
A copy cat!

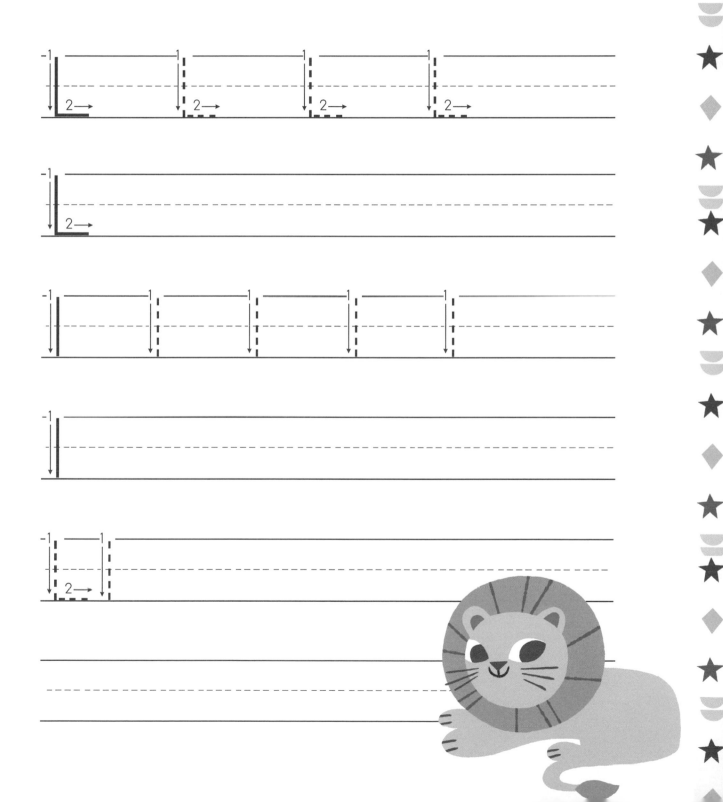

Why do mice need oiling?
Because they squeak!

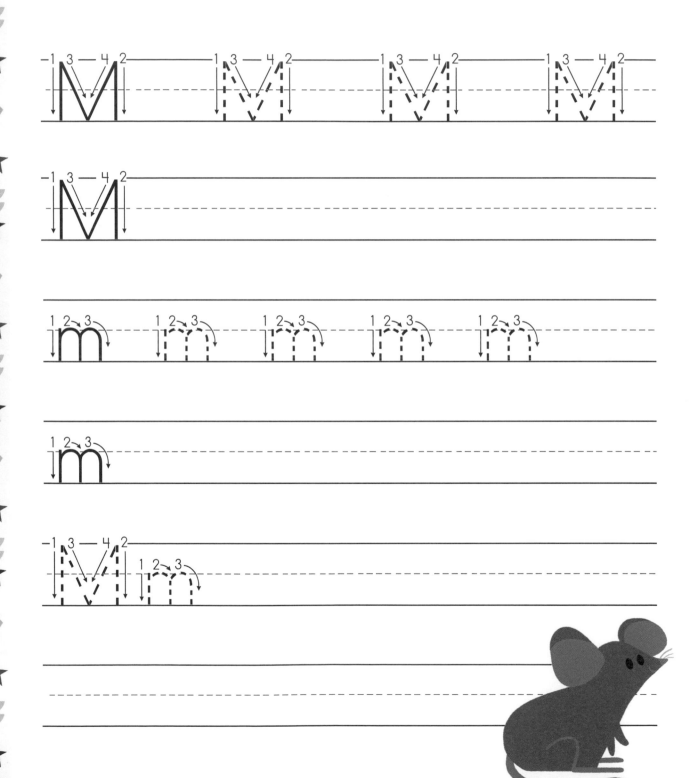

Why is six afraid of seven?
Because seven ate nine!

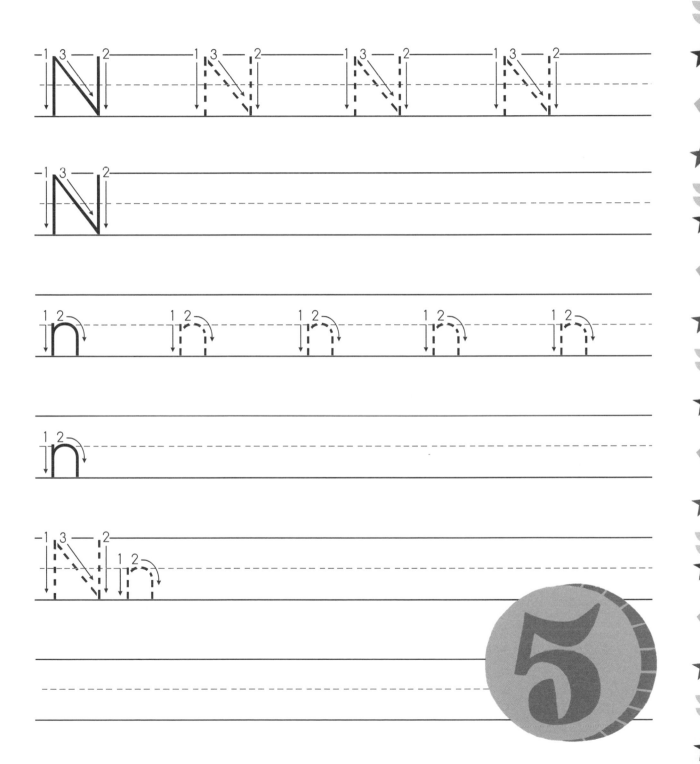

What does an orange sweat?
Orange juice!

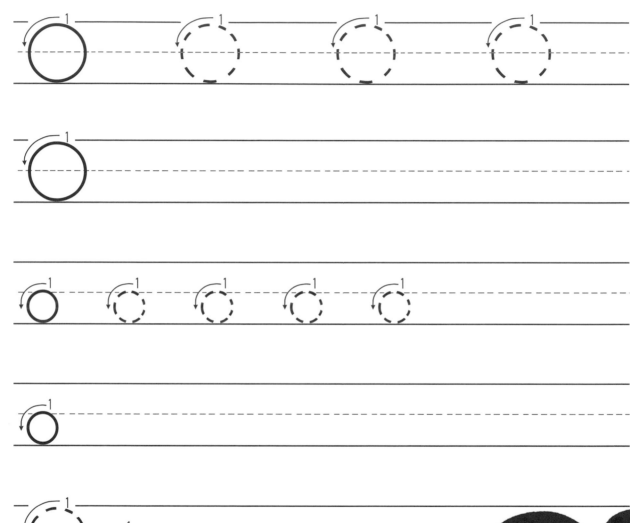

Where do penguins go to the movies?
The dive-in!

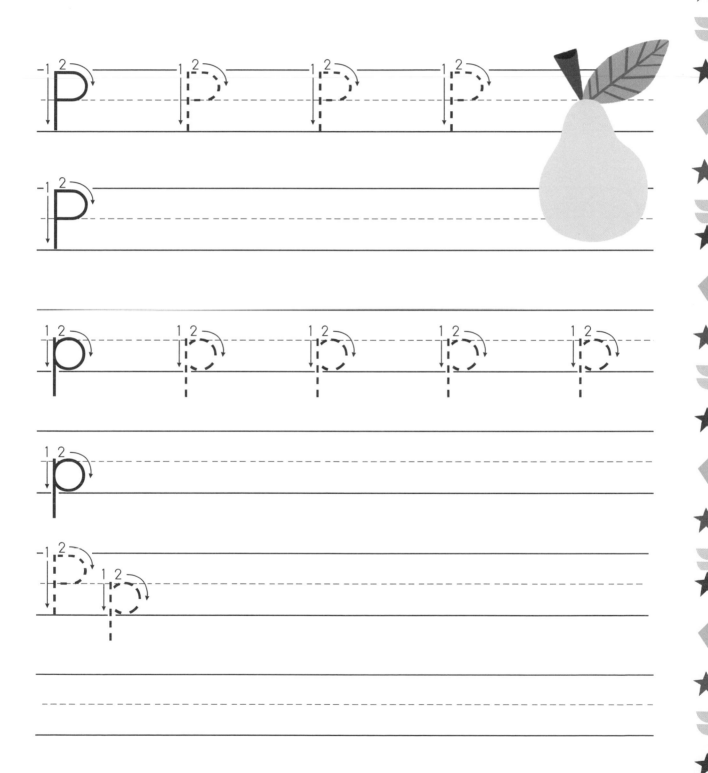

Why did the football coach go to the bank?
To get his quarter back!

How does the rain tie its shoes?
With a rainbow!

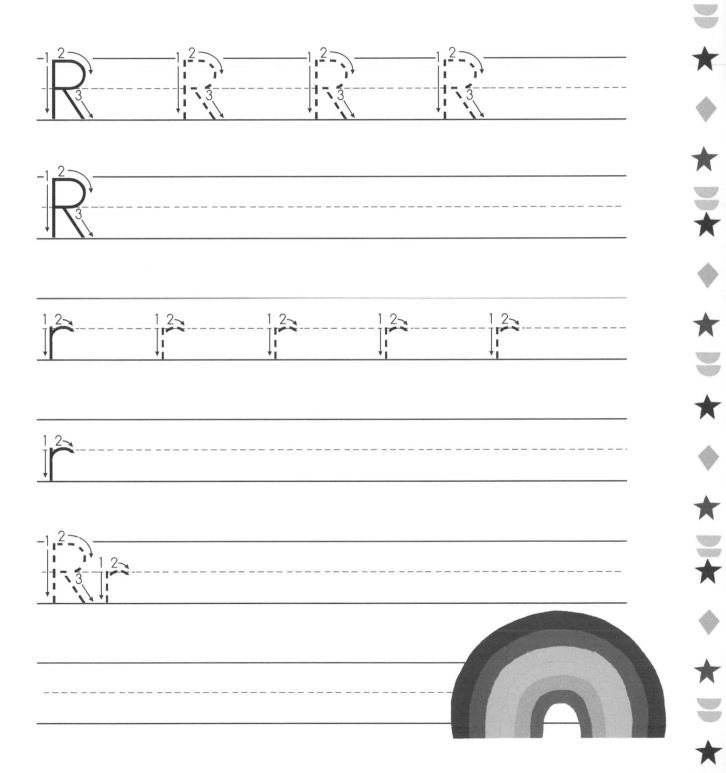

How do snails make important calls?
On shell phones!

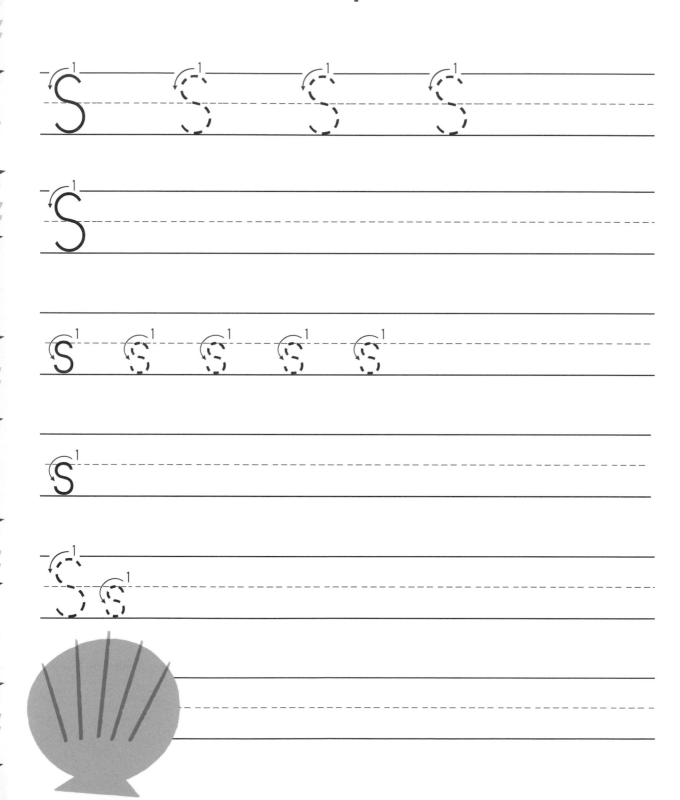

What's the fiercest flower in the garden?
The tiger lily!

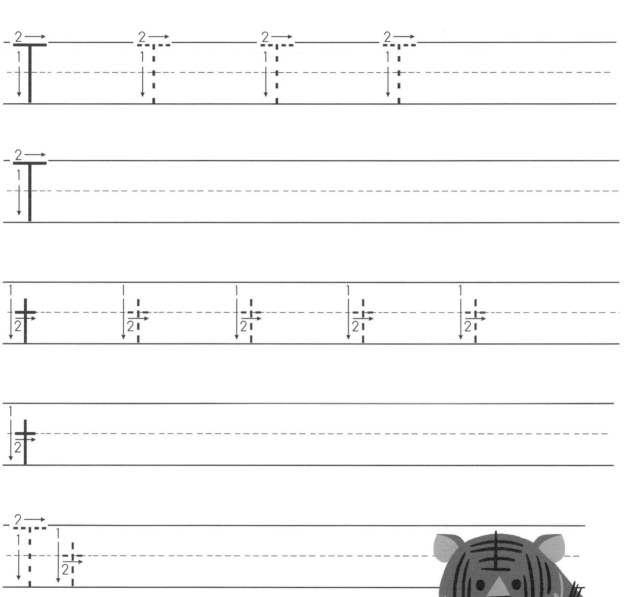

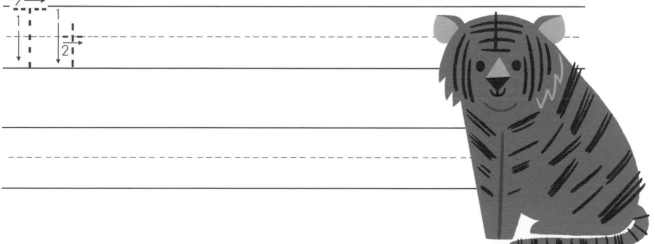

What do unicorns call their dad?
Pop corn!

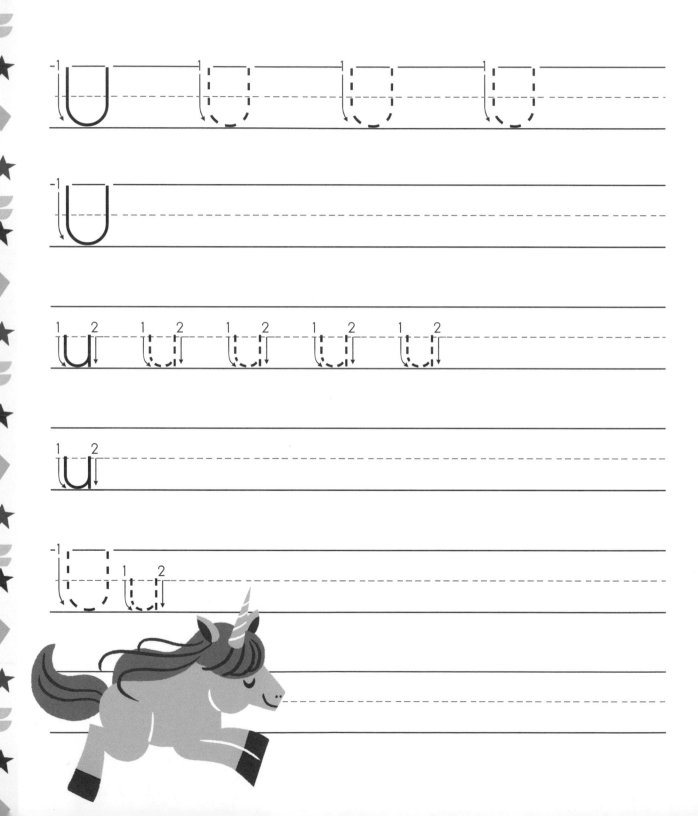

What did one volcano say to another?
I lava you!

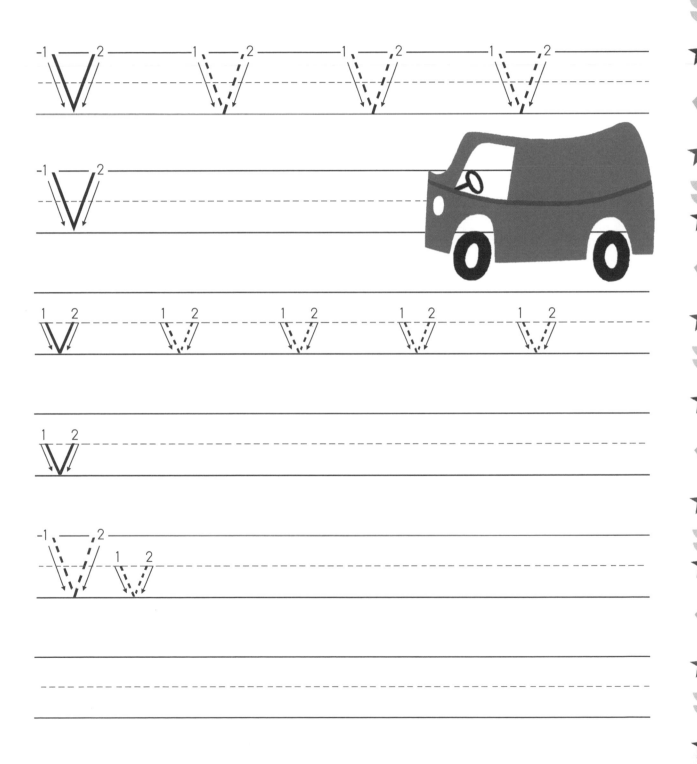

What is the laziest part of the car?
The wheels, because they're always tired!

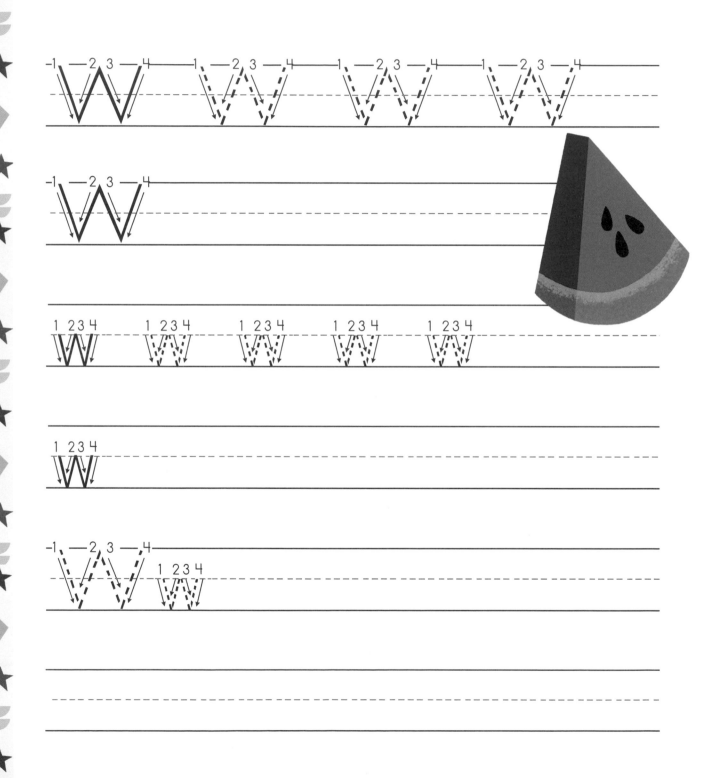

What do you call an X-ray?
A skelfie!

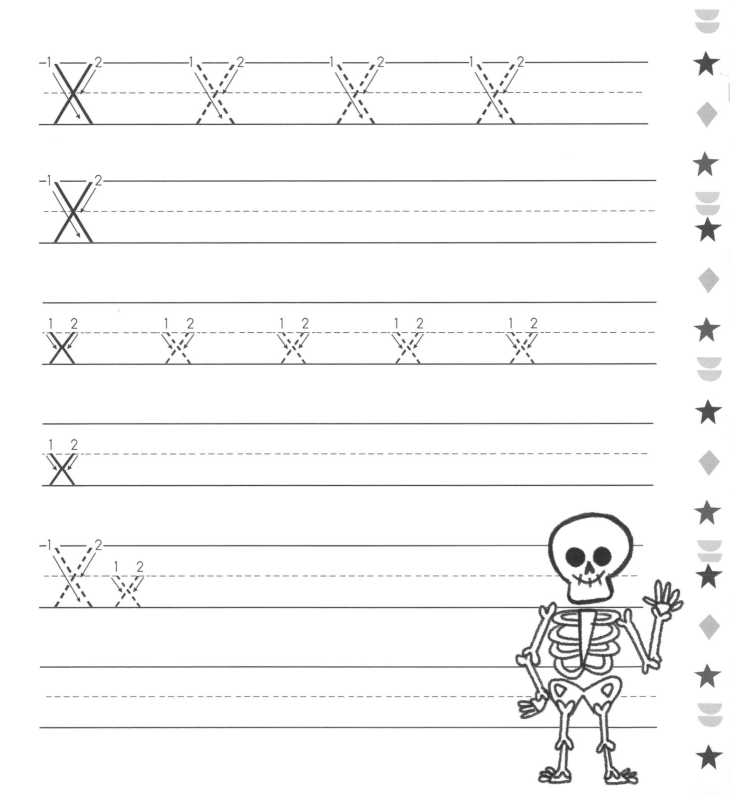

Why can't you tease egg whites?
They can't take a yolk!

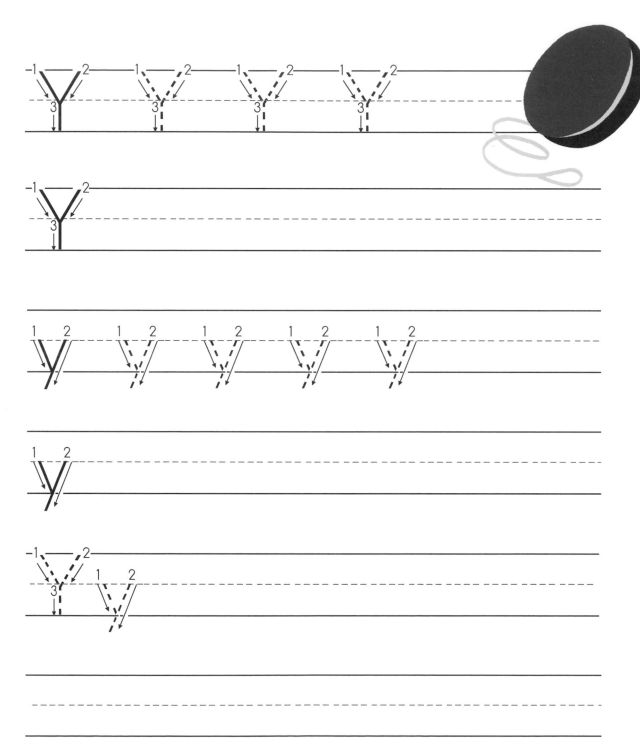

What's black, white, and red all over?
A zebra with a sunburn!

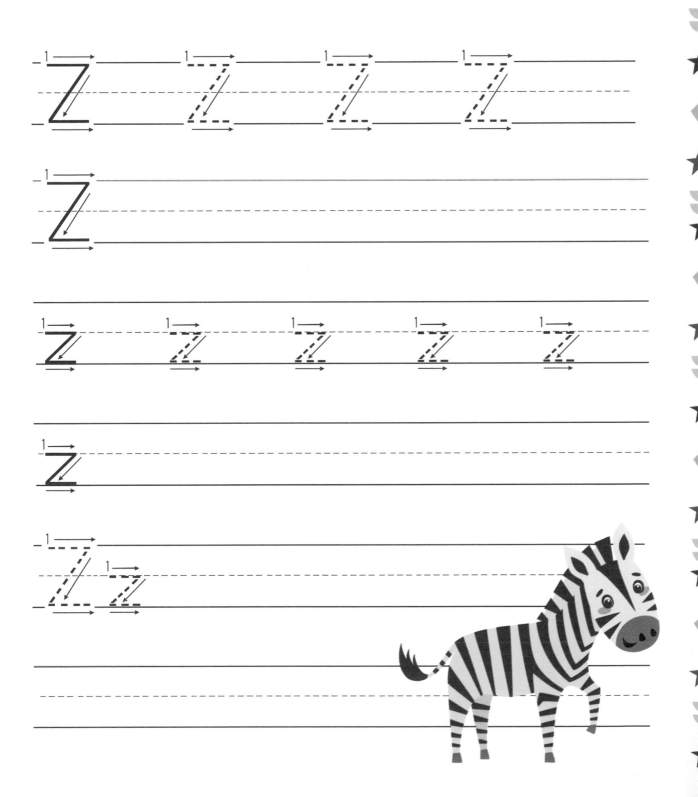

Trace and Write Words

DIRECTIONS

Way to go! You have learned to write the alphabet in print. Now, let's practice combining letters to create words. On each page, you will learn to write four different words that can be found in the joke at the top.

To begin, trace each word and then write each one on your own. Use the space provided to write each word as many times as you can. If you feel confident, try writing with a pen.

Pay attention to the first word on every line. It will include numbers and arrows to help you remember how to write each letter.

You are doing great!

Happy writing!

What do you call a dinosaur that is sleeping?
A dino-snore!

What did the dalmatian say after lunch?
That hit the spot!

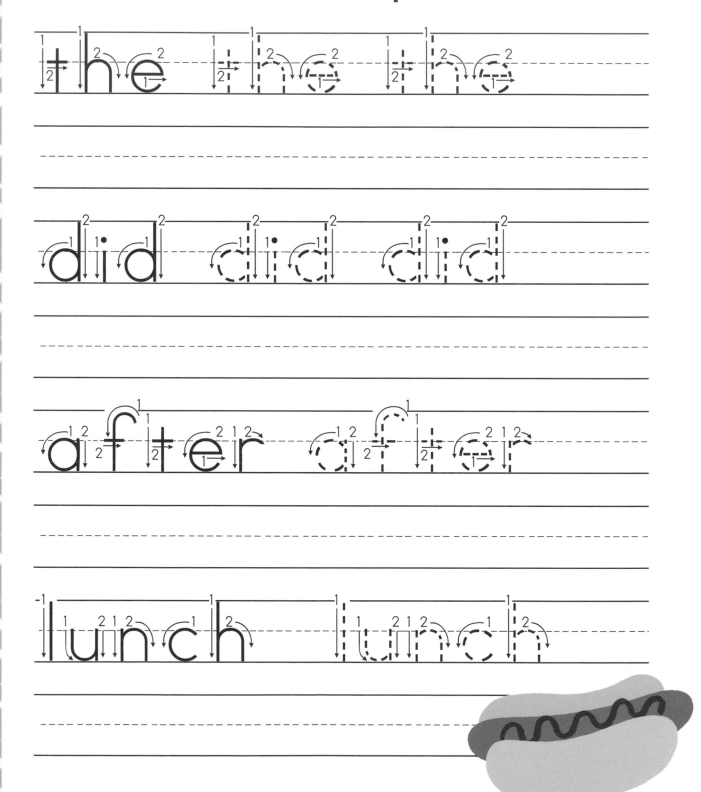

How do you stop an astronaut's baby from crying?
You rocket!

do   do   do

how how how

stop stop stop

rocket rocket

What kind of tree fits in your hand?
A palm tree!

in in in in

of of of of

tree tree

hand hand

Why did the cookie go to the hospital?
Because it felt crummy!

go go go

why why why

felt felt felt

cookie cookie

How do you talk to a giant?
Use big words!

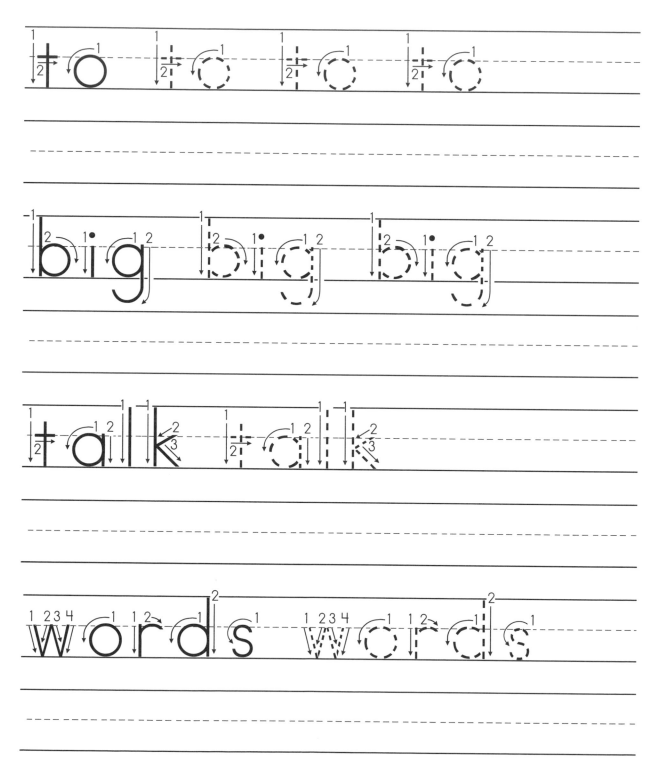

What falls in winter but never gets hurt?
Snow!

How do we know that the ocean is friendly?
It waves!

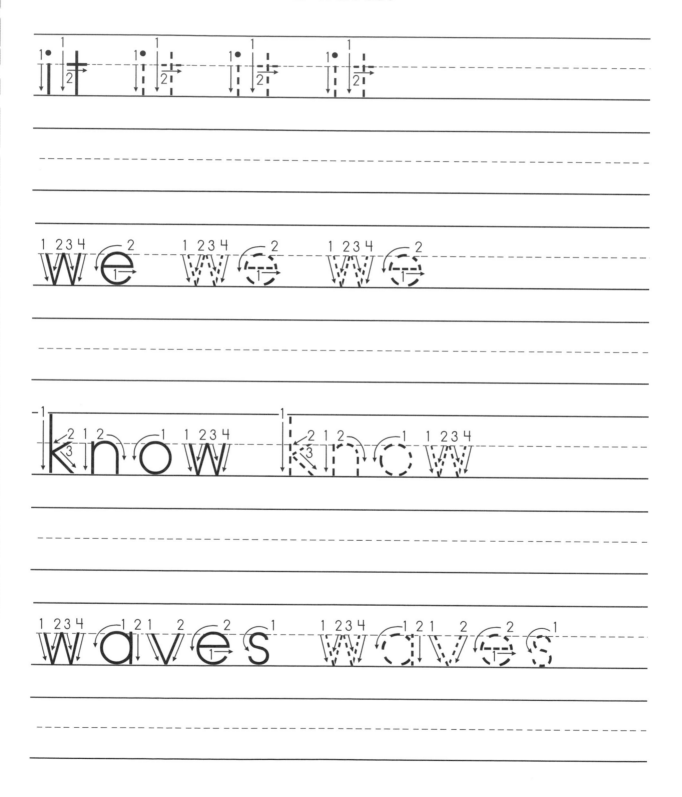

How does the moon cut his hair?
Eclipse it!

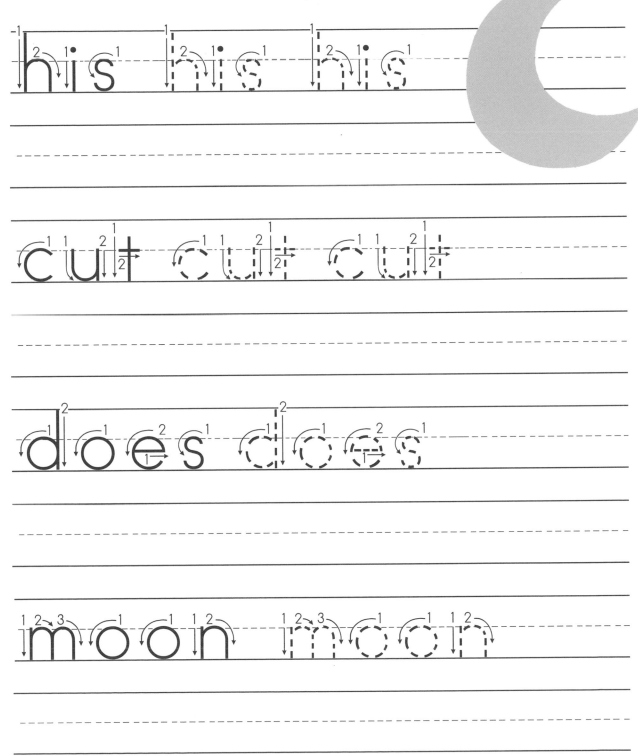

How do you get a squirrel to like you?
Act like a nut!

get get get

act act act

nut nut nut

squirrel squirrel

How do you make an octopus laugh?
With ten-tickles!

How do you make a tissue dance?
Put a little boogie in it!

Why didn't the skeleton go to the dance?
He had no body to dance with!

no no no

body body

with with

skeleton skeleton

What do you call a bear with no teeth?
A gummy bear!

what what

bear bear

teeth teeth

gummy gummy

What do you call a pig that knows karate?
A pork chop!

do do do

chop chop chop

pig pig pig

karate karate

What animal needs to wear a wig?
A bald eagle!

wig wig

wear wear

bald bald

eagle eagle

Why do bees have sticky hair?
Because they use honey combs!

use use use

bees bees

hair hair

combs combs

What do you call an alligator in a vest?
An investigator!

What did one hat say to the other?
Stay here, I'm going on ahead!

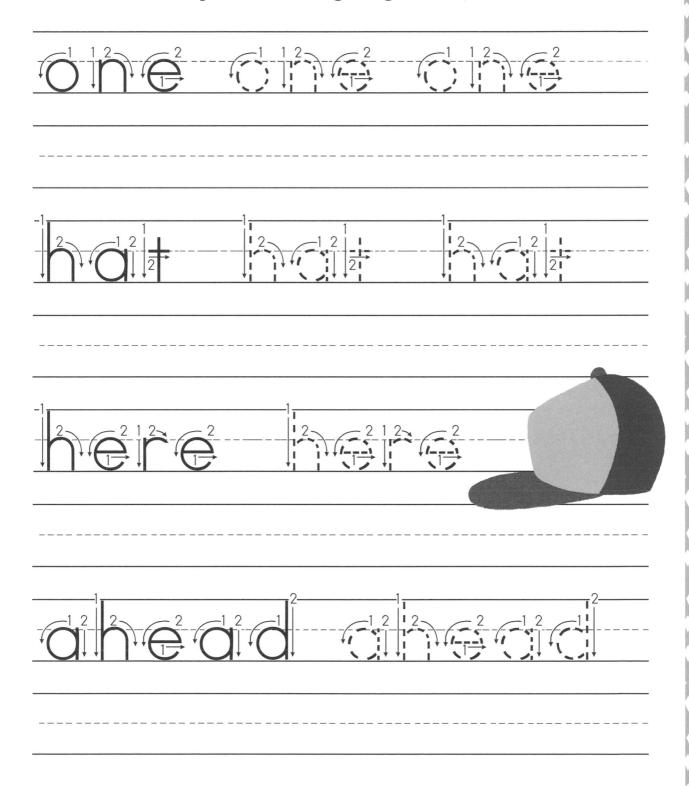

What kind of shoes do ninjas wear?
Sneakers!

kind kind

shoes shoes

wear wear

ninjas ninjas

Why is it dangerous to play cards in the jungle?
Because there are so many cheetahs!

are are are

many many

cards cards

jungle jungle

What do you call a puppy stuck in the rain?
A soggy doggy!

rain rain

stuck stuck

puppy puppy

doggy doggy

Trace and Write Jokes

▲▽▲▽▲▽▲▽▲▽▲▽▲▽▲▽▲▽▲▽▲▽▲▽▲▽▲▽▲▽▲

DIRECTIONS

Great job on writing so many words! You should be proud of yourself. Let's keeping going and have a little more fun.

Throughout this book, you have learned a lot of jokes and had a few good laughs. In this section, you will practice tracing and writing jokes. For the first half of this section, read the joke question and trace the answer. Then, for the second half of this section, you will read the joke question and answer, and then write the joke in your best print handwriting. You can color the pictures, too!

Get ready to laugh, and make sure you share these jokes later with your friends. Enjoy this hilarious handwriting activity!

Happy writing
(and laughing)!

What is the Easter Bunny's favorite restaurant?

▲▽▲▽▲▽▲▽▲▽▲▽▲▽▲▽▲▽▲▽

IHOP!

What do you call a monkey that loves potato chips?

▲▼▲▼▲▼▲▼▲▼▲▼▲▼▲▼▲▼▲▼

A chipmonk!

Why was the broom late?

▽▲▽▲▽▲▽▲▽▲▽▲▽▲▽▲▽

It over swept!

Why did the banana go to the doctor?

▽▲▽▲▽▲▽▲▽▲▽▲▽▲▽▲▽▲▽▲▽

It wasn't peeling well!

What do you call two birds in love?

▲▽▲▽▲▽▲▽▲▽▲▽▲▽▲▽▲▽▲▽▲▽

Tweet-hearts!

Why did the math book look so sad?

▲▽▲▽▲▽▲▽▲▽▲▽▲▽▲▽▲▽

Because it had so many problems!

What do you
get from a
cow that gets
her own way
all the time?

▲▽▲▲▽▲▽▲▽▲▽▲▽▲▽▲▽▲▽

Spoiled milk!

What did one eye say to the other eye?

▲▽▲▽▲▽▲▽▲▽▲▽▲▽▲▽▲▽▲▽▲▽

Don't look now, but something between us smells!

Why can't your nose be twelve inches long?

▲▼▲▼▲▼▲▼▲▼▲▼▲▼▲▼

Because then it would be a foot!

Why did the
police officer
give the sheep
a ticket?

▲▽▲▽▲▽▲▽▲▽▲▽▲▽▲▽▲▽▲▽

Because he
was a baaa-d
driver!

Why does Humpty Dumpty like autumn?

▲▼▲▼▲▼▲▼▲▼▲▼▲▼▲▼▲▼▲▼

Because he had a great fall!

Where do fish keep their money?
In the river bank!

Write the joke in your best print. Try your best!

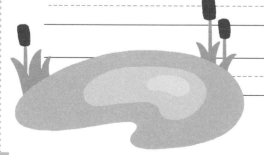

Where do sheep go on vacation?

To the Baaaa-hamas!

Write the joke in your best print. Try your best!

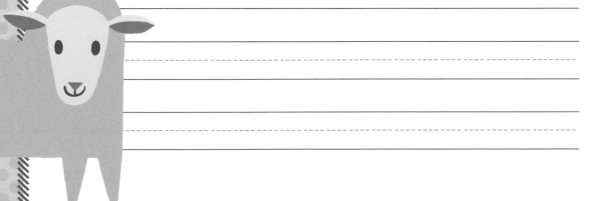

Where do monkeys exercise?

At the jungle gym!

Write the joke in your best print. Try your best!

What do cats eat for breakfast? Mice crispies!

Write the joke in your best print. Try your best!

What do fish play on the piano?
Scales!

Write the joke in your best print. Try your best!

_____

- -

_____

- -

_____

- -

_____

- -

_____

- -

_____

What is the smartest kind of bee?

A spelling bee!

Write the joke in your best print. Try your best!

_____

- -

_____

_____

- -

_____

_____

- -

_____

_____

- -

_____

What do you call cheese that isn't yours?
Nacho cheese!

Write the joke in your best print. Try your best!

_____
- - - - - - - - - - - - - - - - -
_____

_____
- - - - - - - - - - - - - - - - -
_____

_____
- - - - - - - - - - - - - - - - -
_____

_____
- - - - - - - - - - - - - - - - -
_____

Where do cows go for entertainment?
The moo-vies!

Write the joke in your best print. Try your best!

_____
- -
_____

_____
- -
_____

_____
- -
_____

_____
- -
_____

_____
- -
_____

What do you call a sleeping bull?
A bull dozer!

Write the joke in your best print. Try your best!

_____

- -

_____

_____

- -

_____

_____

- -

_____

_____

- -

_____

_____

- -

_____

Why did the picture go to jail?
It was framed!

Write the joke in your best print. Try your best!

What has hands but can't clap?

A clock!

Write the joke in your best print. Try your best!

_____
- - - - - - - - - - - - - - - - - - - -
_____

_____
- - - - - - - - - - - - - - - - - - - -
_____

_____
- - - - - - - - - - - - - - - - - - - -
_____

_____
- - - - - - - - - - - - - - - - - - - -
_____

_____
- - - - - - - - - - - - - - - - - - - -
_____

What do you call fake noodles?

Im-pasta!

Write the joke in your best print. Try your best!

_____
- -
_____

_____
- -
_____

_____
- -
_____

_____
- -
_____

_____
- -
_____

Certificate of Completion

This certificate is presented to

_ _

for learning to write in print!

Date _____

About the Author

Crystal Radke is an educational leader, speaker, and writer. After spending time as a classroom teacher, she began her consultant business, where she mentors educators by providing inspirational keynotes and powerful professional development. Her degrees in education and experience as a foster and adoptive mother have made helping children learn and grow a personal mission.